Threat Hunting with Splunk: Practical Techniques and APT Detection

Omar Borg

Published by Omar Borg, 2023.

Table of Contents

Title: Threat Hunting with Splunk: Practical Techniques and APT Detection

Table of Contents

Introduction

Mastering Security and Compliance with Splunk

In an increasingly interconnected and digitized world, the significance of robust cybersecurity and unwavering compliance cannot be overstated. Organizations of all sizes face a multitude of threats, from sophisticated cyberattacks to regulatory complexities that demand diligence and vigilance. In this era where data reigns supreme, safeguarding sensitive information and ensuring adherence to industry standards and regulations have become paramount.

This book embarks on a comprehensive journey through the intricate landscape of cybersecurity, threat detection, incident response, and compliance monitoring, all with one powerful ally at the center: Splunk. Splunk, a versatile data analysis and visualization platform, is a game-changer in the realm of security and compliance. With its capabilities to collect, analyze, and act upon vast amounts of data from various sources, Splunk empowers organizations to protect their digital assets, respond swiftly to security incidents, and maintain the highest standards of compliance.

Our exploration begins with the foundations of cybersecurity, delving into the evolving threat landscape and the fundamental principles that underpin security practices. From there, we venture into the world of threat hunting, where we learn to proactively seek out and combat potential security threats using Splunk's powerful tools.

As we progress, we unveil the potent combination of Yara rules and threat intelligence sharing, equipping you with the means to identify and combat malware and advanced persistent threats (APTs). Through practical examples and real-world use cases, you'll master the art of crafting Yara rules and leveraging threat intelligence to bolster your defenses.

Splunk's capabilities shine further as we explore its role in incident response, security automation, and orchestration. Discover how Splunk can be your guiding light in navigating the complexities of incident management, allowing you to detect, respond to, and remediate security incidents with precision and efficiency.

No modern organization can overlook the imperative of compliance. With Splunk, you'll journey through the intricate terrain of compliance monitoring, understanding how to maintain adherence to a multitude of regulations and frameworks, from PCI DSS to GDPR. Splunk's real-time data analysis and reporting prowess ensure that your compliance efforts remain not just efficient but also auditable and robust.

As you navigate these chapters, you'll encounter practical examples, hands-on guidance, and real-world scenarios that illuminate the path to mastering security and compliance with Splunk. Whether you're a seasoned security professional or just embarking on your cybersecurity journey, this book will equip you with the knowledge and tools needed to protect your organization's digital assets, ensure compliance, and thrive in an ever-evolving digital landscape.

Join us as we unlock the full potential of Splunk and embark on this transformative journey to safeguard your organization and navigate the intricacies of modern security and compliance.

About This Book

"Mastering Security and Compliance with Splunk" is your comprehensive guide to leveraging the power of Splunk, a versatile data analysis and visualization platform, to fortify your organization's cybersecurity defenses and navigate the complexities of compliance effectively. Whether you are a seasoned security professional, an IT administrator, or just embarking on your cybersecurity journey, this book equips you with the knowledge and practical skills needed to safeguard your digital assets, respond to security incidents, and ensure compliance with industry standards and regulations.

Who Is This Book For?

This book is designed for a wide range of readers, including:

Security Professionals: Gain insights into using Splunk as a central tool for threat detection, incident response, and compliance monitoring. Discover advanced techniques and best practices to bolster your organization's security posture.

IT Administrators: Learn how to harness Splunk's capabilities to monitor and protect your organization's network, systems, and data. Implement practical solutions to enhance security and streamline compliance efforts.

Compliance Officers: Understand how Splunk can simplify compliance monitoring and reporting across various regulatory frameworks, enabling your organization to maintain adherence to industry standards.

Splunk Enthusiasts: If you are new to Splunk, this book provides a structured introduction to its features and capabilities, with a focus on security and compliance use cases.

What You Will Learn

Foundations of Cybersecurity: Explore the principles of cybersecurity, the evolving threat landscape, and the essential components of a robust security strategy.

Threat Detection and Hunting: Master the art of threat hunting using Splunk, proactively identifying and mitigating security threats before they escalate.

Yara Rules and Threat Intelligence: Craft Yara rules and harness the power of threat intelligence sharing to detect and combat malware and advanced persistent threats (APTs).

Incident Response: Develop effective incident response strategies and automate incident management workflows using Splunk.

Security Automation and Orchestration: Implement automation and orchestration techniques to streamline security operations and respond to threats with precision.

Compliance Monitoring: Navigate the intricate landscape of compliance, from PCI DSS to GDPR, using Splunk's real-time data analysis and reporting capabilities.

Why This Book Matters

In today's interconnected world, cybersecurity and compliance are non-negotiable aspects of every organization's success. A security breach can result in financial losses, damage to reputation, and legal ramifications. Non-compliance with regulations can lead to hefty fines and legal consequences. "Mastering Security and Compliance with Splunk" empowers you with the knowledge and skills to protect your organization, respond effectively to incidents, and ensure adherence to industry standards.

What You Need

To get the most out of this book, you will need access to a Splunk environment. Whether you are using Splunk Enterprise, Splunk Cloud, or Splunk Light, the principles and techniques discussed in this book can be applied to various Splunk deployments. Additionally, a basic understanding of cybersecurity concepts and familiarity with IT infrastructure will be beneficial.

Let's Get Started

Embark on this educational journey to become a Splunk expert, fortify your organization's security posture, and navigate the intricate world of compliance with confidence. "Mastering Security and Compliance with Splunk" is your indispensable companion on this quest to safeguard your digital assets and ensure compliance in an ever-evolving digital landscape.

Chapter 1: Setting Up Your Threat Hunting Environment

- Installing and Configuring Splunk
- Data Collection: Logs and Sources
- Building a Threat Hunting Dashboard

Chapter 2: Basic Splunk Commands

- Introduction to Splunk Search Language (SPL)

- Searching and Filtering Data

- Time Range and Indexing

- Field Extraction

- Aggregations and Stats

- Advanced Searching Techniques

Chapter 3: Building Your Threat Hunting Queries

- Writing Effective Queries

- Analyzing Log Data

- Creating Alerts

- Threat Hunting Use Cases

- Detecting Suspicious Activity

- Identifying Anomalies

- Hunting for IoCs

- Tracking Lateral Movement

Chapter 4: Practical Examples of Threat Hunting

- Example 1: Detecting Unauthorized Access Attempts

- Example 2: Identifying Data Exfiltration

- Example 3: Investigating Phishing Campaigns

- Example 4: Uncovering Insider Threats

- Example 5: Advanced Threat Detection with Machine Learning

Chapter 5: Threat Intelligence and APTs

- What are Advanced Persistent Threats (APTs)?
- The Top 10 Known APT Groups
- Indicators of Compromise (IoCs)
- Using Threat Intelligence Feeds
- Incorporating Threat Feeds into Splunk

Chapter 6: Hunting for APTs

- Practical Examples of APT Hunting
- APT1 (Comment Crew)
- APT28 (Fancy Bear)
- APT29 (Cozy Bear)
- APT32 (OceanBuffalo)
- APT33 (Elfin)
- APT34 (OilRig)
- APT35 (Charming Kitten)
- APT41 (Double Dragon)
- APT40 (Leviathan)
- APT-C-23 (APT23)

Chapter 7: Advanced Threat Hunting Techniques

- Using YARA Rules

- Analyzing Network Traffic

- Analyzing Memory Dumps

- Incorporating Threat Intelligence

Chapter 8: Incident Response and Remediation

- Responding to Threats

- Containment and Isolation

- Eradication and Recovery

- Documentation and Post-Incident Review

Chapter 9: Best Practices and Pitfalls to Avoid

- Best Practices for Threat Hunting
- Common Pitfalls and Mistakes

Chapter 10: The Future of Threat Hunting

- Emerging Threats and Challenges

- Automation and AI in Threat Hunting

- Continuous Improvement and Training

Conclusion

- Recap of Key Concepts

- The Ongoing Journey of Threat Hunting

- Resources and Further Reading

- Appendix A: Splunk Search Commands Cheat Sheet

- Essential Splunk Commands and Examples

- Appendix B: Threat Hunting Toolkit

- Useful Tools and Resources for Threat Hunters

- Index

This book will guide you through the process of setting up a threat hunting environment using Splunk and provide practical examples of how to detect and investigate threats. It will also delve into the world of Advanced Persistent Threats (APTs) and offer examples of known APT groups and their Indicators of Compromise (IoCs). Armed with this knowledge and hands-on experience, you'll be better equipped to proactively defend your organization against cyber threats.

Chapter 1: Setting Up Your Threat Hunting Environment

In the world of threat hunting, success starts with having the right tools and a well-prepared environment. This chapter will walk you through the essential steps to set up your threat hunting environment using Splunk, ensuring you have a solid foundation for effective threat detection and investigation.

1.1 Installing and Configuring Splunk

Before you can begin hunting for threats, you need to install and configure Splunk, one of the most powerful and widely used security information and event management (SIEM) tools available.

1.1.1 Installation

Splunk offers both a free version called Splunk Enterprise Free and a paid version called Splunk Enterprise. The installation process is similar for both.

Visit the Splunk website (www.splunk.com) and download the appropriate version for your operating system.

Follow the installation instructions provided for your platform. You'll be guided through the installation wizard, where you can choose the installation directory, port settings, and other configurations.

Once Splunk is installed, start the Splunk service. You can usually do this from the command line or using the Splunk Manager interface.

1.1.2 Configuration

After installation, you'll need to configure Splunk to meet your threat hunting needs:

Set up data inputs: Configure Splunk to collect data from various sources, such as logs, network traffic, and more. Splunk supports a wide range of data sources, and you can specify how and where data should be collected.

Define indexes: Create indexes to organize and categorize your data. Proper indexing is crucial for efficient searching and analysis.

Configure user access: Control who can access your Splunk instance and what level of access they have. Ensure that only authorized personnel can access sensitive data.

Install and configure apps and add-ons: Splunk has a vibrant ecosystem of apps and add-ons that extend its capabilities. Depending on your specific needs, you may want to install security-related apps and add-ons to enhance your threat hunting capabilities.

1.2 Data Collection: Logs and Sources

Effective threat hunting relies on collecting and analyzing data from a variety of sources within your environment. Here are some key data sources to consider:

System Logs: Collect logs from servers, workstations, and other devices. These logs can provide valuable information about system activities, logins, and potential security incidents.

Network Traffic: Capture network traffic data using tools like Wireshark or by configuring network appliances to send logs to Splunk. Network data can help identify suspicious communications and potential threats.

Security Devices: Integrate security appliances such as firewalls, intrusion detection systems (IDS), and antivirus solutions with Splunk. These devices generate logs that can be crucial for threat detection.

Application Logs: Many applications generate logs that can be useful for identifying abnormal behavior or unauthorized access. Ensure that critical applications are configured to log relevant events.

Cloud Services: If your organization uses cloud services like AWS, Azure, or GCP, configure log forwarding to Splunk to monitor cloud activity and detect anomalies.

1.3 Building a Threat Hunting Dashboard

A well-organized and informative dashboard is a vital tool for threat hunters. It provides an at-a-glance view of the current security posture and enables you to quickly identify potential issues. Here's how to build an effective threat hunting dashboard in Splunk:

Identify Key Metrics: Determine which security metrics are most important for your organization. These could include login attempts, firewall events, failed authentication, and more.

Create Visualizations: Use Splunk's visualization capabilities to create charts, graphs, and tables that display relevant security data. Visualizations make it easier to spot trends and anomalies.

Set Up Alerts: Configure alerts to notify you when specific events or conditions occur. Alerts can be based on threshold values or predefined rules, allowing you to respond swiftly to potential threats.

Customize the Dashboard: Tailor your dashboard to your organization's needs. You may want to create different dashboards for different teams or focus areas within threat hunting.

Regularly Update and Refine: Threat landscapes change constantly, so your dashboard should evolve with them. Regularly review and update your dashboard to ensure it remains effective in detecting new threats.

By the end of this chapter, you'll have Splunk installed, configured, and ready to start collecting data from various sources within your environment. With a well-designed dashboard in place, you'll be well-prepared to embark on your threat hunting journey. In the following chapters, we'll delve into the essential Splunk commands and techniques needed to uncover threats and detect suspicious activity in your data.

Chapter 2: Basic Splunk Commands

In Chapter 1, you learned how to set up your threat hunting environment using Splunk. Now, let's dive into the fundamentals of using Splunk for threat hunting. This chapter will introduce you to the essential Splunk commands and techniques that will empower you to search, filter, and analyze your data effectively.

2.1 Introduction to Splunk Search Language (SPL)

Splunk's search language, known as SPL, is a powerful tool for querying and analyzing data. It allows you to extract insights from your data by using a combination of search commands, functions, and keywords. Here are some core concepts:

Search Head: The component of Splunk that processes search requests and displays the results. This is where you'll run your SPL queries.

Index: A collection of data that you've configured Splunk to monitor. Data is stored in indexes, and you can have multiple indexes for different types of data.

Event: A single line of data in Splunk, often corresponding to a log entry.

2.2 Searching and Filtering Data

In this section, you'll learn the basic commands for searching and filtering data:

search: The fundamental command for searching data. You can use it to search for specific keywords or patterns in your data.

| (pipe): Used to chain commands together. You can filter and manipulate data by chaining multiple commands.

fields: Allows you to specify which fields to display in the search results. This is useful for focusing on relevant information.

2.3 Time Range and Indexing

Time is a critical aspect of threat hunting. You'll often need to analyze data over specific time ranges and correlate events. Here's how you can work with time in Splunk:

earliest and latest: Define a time range for your search by specifying the earliest and latest times. For example, you can search for events in the last 24 hours using **earliest=-24h@h latest=now.**

index: Use the index command to search within a specific index. This is helpful when you have multiple indexes and want to narrow down your search.

2.4 Field Extraction

Effective threat hunting often requires extracting meaningful fields from your data. Splunk provides several methods for field extraction:

rex: Use regular expressions with the rex command to extract fields from unstructured data.

kv: Extract key-value pairs from data using the kv command.

field=value extraction: Define custom field extractions in Splunk's configuration files or directly in your search query.

2.5 Aggregations and Stats

To gain insights from your data, you'll frequently need to aggregate and summarize information. Splunk offers commands for this purpose:

stats: Perform statistical operations like count, sum, and average on your data.

count: Count the number of events that match your search criteria.

top: Find the top values for a specific field in your data.

2.6 Advanced Searching Techniques

This section will cover advanced search techniques and commands that are valuable for threat hunting:

eval: Create calculated fields and perform mathematical operations on your data.

join: Merge data from multiple sources based on common fields.

dedup: Remove duplicate events from your search results.

transaction: Group related events together to analyze them as a single unit.

By the end of this chapter, you'll have a solid grasp of the basic Splunk commands and techniques necessary to start searching and filtering data effectively. These skills are the foundation for more advanced threat hunting queries and will enable you to uncover suspicious activity and potential threats in your data. In the subsequent chapters, you'll explore practical examples of threat hunting scenarios and how to apply these commands in real-world situations.

Chapter 3: Building Your Threat Hunting Queries

Now that you have a foundational understanding of Splunk's basic commands, it's time to apply this knowledge to create effective threat hunting queries. In this chapter, you'll learn how to craft queries that enable you to detect suspicious activities, identify anomalies, and hunt for Indicators of Compromise (IoCs).

3.1 Writing Effective Queries

Writing effective queries is essential for successful threat hunting. A well-crafted query can help you quickly pinpoint potential threats. Here are some best practices:

Be Specific: Clearly define your search criteria. Use keywords, field names, and time ranges to narrow down your search.

Use Boolean Operators: Splunk supports Boolean operators like AND, OR, and NOT. Combine them to refine your searches.

Leverage Wildcards: Use wildcard characters like *** and ?** to match patterns within your data. For example, **user=*admin*** matches usernames containing **"admin."**

3.2 Analyzing Log Data

Log data is a valuable source of information for threat hunting. In this section, you'll learn how to analyze log data effectively:

Log Sources: Understand the different types of logs generated by systems, applications, and devices in your environment.

Log Parsing: Use field extractions and regular expressions to parse log data and extract relevant information.

Correlation: Look for patterns and correlations between different log entries to identify potential threats.

3.3 Creating Alerts

Creating alerts allows you to proactively detect and respond to suspicious activities. Learn how to set up alerts based on predefined rules or threshold values. Examples include:

Alerting on multiple failed login attempts within a short time frame.

Alerting when a user accesses sensitive data or systems outside of business hours.

3.4 Threat Hunting Use Cases

In this section, we'll explore practical threat hunting use cases and how to approach them using Splunk:

Detecting Suspicious Activity: Craft queries to detect known malicious patterns, such as repeated failed login attempts or unusual network traffic.

Identifying Anomalies: Use statistical analysis and anomaly detection techniques to find deviations from normal behavior.

Hunting for IoCs: Search for specific IoCs, such as IP addresses, URLs, or file hashes, within your data. Learn how to use threat intelligence feeds to enhance your IoC hunting.

Tracking Lateral Movement: Investigate potential lateral movement within your network. Identify unusual account activity and connections between systems.

3.5 Practical Examples of Threat Hunting

This section will provide you with hands-on examples of threat hunting scenarios, including step-by-step guides on crafting queries and interpreting results. Examples include:

Example 1: Detecting Suspicious Account Activity

Example 2: Identifying Data Exfiltration

Example 3: Investigating Phishing Campaigns

Example 4: Uncovering Insider Threats

Example 5: Advanced Threat Detection with Machine Learning

Chapter 4: Practical Examples of Threat Hunting

In this chapter, we will explore practical examples of threat hunting scenarios, providing step-by-step guidance on how to craft queries, analyze results, and interpret findings using Splunk. Each example focuses on detecting and investigating potential security threats within your environment.

Example 1: Detecting Suspicious Account Activity

Scenario: You want to identify suspicious account activity, such as multiple failed login attempts from the same IP address within a short time frame.

Step 1: Craft a Splunk Query

spl

index=security_logs source="authentication.log"

| stats count by user, src_ip

| where count > 5

Step 2: Interpret the Results

This query searches the **"authentication.log"** data for patterns of failed login attempts.

It groups results by the user and the **source IP address**.

The where **count > 5** filter identifies instances where there have been more than 5 failed login attempts from the same **IP address**.

Review the results to identify potentially **suspicious IP addresses** and **users with repeated failed login attempts**.

Example 2: Identifying Data Exfiltration

Scenario: You suspect **data exfiltration** and want to detect large or unusual data transfers leaving your network.

Step 1: Craft a Splunk Query

spl

index=network_logs action="outbound" bytes_out > 1000000

Step 2: Interpret the Results

This query searches network logs for outbound traffic with data transfers exceeding 1 MB.

It focuses on **"action=outbound"** events, which typically indicate data leaving your network.

Review the results to identify large or **unusual outbound data transfers** that may require further investigation.

Example 3: Investigating Phishing Campaigns

Scenario: You've received reports of **suspicious emails**, and you want to investigate whether there's an ongoing **phishing campaign**.

Step 1: Craft a Splunk Query

spl

index=email_logs sourcetype="email"

| search subject="Important Account Verification"

| stats count by sender, recipient

Step 2: Interpret the Results

This query searches email logs for emails with the **subject line "Important Account Verification."**

It provides a count of these emails grouped by sender and recipient.

Review the results to identify **patterns or anomalies** in email communication that might indicate a **phishing campaign**.

Example 4: Uncovering Insider Threats

Scenario: You want to **detect insider threats** by monitoring unusual behavior from employees with access to sensitive data.

Step 1: Craft a Splunk Query

spl

index=access_logs action="access" sensitive_data="true"

| stats count by user, action

| where count > 10 AND action="delete"

_____

Step 2: Interpret the Results

This query searches access logs for **actions related to sensitive data, such as deletions.**

It groups results by the user and the action.

The where **count > 10 AND action="delete" filter identifies users who have deleted sensitive data more than 10 times.**

Review the results to identify users who may be involved in unauthorized data deletions.

_____

Example 5: Advanced Threat Detection with Machine Learning

In this example, we'll delve deeper into leveraging machine learning for advanced threat detection using Splunk. Machine learning models can help you identify anomalies and unusual patterns of behavior in your data that might indicate sophisticated threats. Here's a step-by-step guide on how to set up and utilize machine learning for threat hunting in Splunk:

Step 1: Set Up Machine Learning Models

Data Preparation: Before you can use machine learning, ensure that your data is clean, well-structured, and contains historical records. You'll need a dataset that includes features relevant to the threat you're trying to detect.

Install and Configure Machine Learning Toolkit (MLTK): If you haven't already, install the Splunk Machine Learning Toolkit. Configure it to work with your data sources.

Feature Engineering: Identify relevant features in your data that can be used to detect threats. Features could include user behavior, network traffic patterns, or system access logs.

Model Selection: Choose an appropriate machine learning algorithm for your threat detection task. Common choices include clustering algorithms (e.g., k-means) for anomaly detection or supervised learning algorithms (e.g., Random Forest) for classification tasks.

Training Data: Split your historical data into training and testing datasets. The training data is used to train the machine learning model, while the testing data is used to evaluate its performance.

Model Training: Train the machine learning model using the training dataset. Adjust hyperparameters and fine-tune the model for optimal performance.

Step 2: Monitor and Investigate Anomalies

Real-Time Data Ingestion: Configure Splunk to ingest real-time data streams, including logs, network traffic, and system events.

Apply Machine Learning Model: Apply the trained machine learning model to incoming data. This can be done using Splunk's MLTK functionalities.

Anomaly Detection: The machine learning model will generate anomaly scores for each data point. High anomaly scores indicate potential threats or unusual behavior.

Alerting: Set up alerts to trigger notifications when the anomaly scores exceed predefined thresholds. These alerts can be sent to security teams for immediate investigation.

Investigation: When an alert is triggered, security analysts should investigate the anomaly. This involves examining the context of the event, looking at associated logs, and determining whether it represents a genuine threat.

Incident Response: If an anomaly is confirmed as a security threat, initiate the incident response process. This may involve isolating affected systems, remediating the threat, and documenting the incident.

Feedback Loop: Continuously update and retrain your machine learning models based on new threat data and evolving attack techniques. The feedback loop ensures that your models remain effective over time.

Example Use Cases for Machine Learning in Threat Detection:

User and Entity Behavior Analytics (UEBA): Build models that detect unusual user or entity behavior, such as privileged account abuse or data exfiltration.

Network Anomaly Detection: Utilize machine learning to identify network anomalies, such as port scans, lateral movement, or DNS tunneling.

Malware Detection: Train models to detect previously unknown malware based on file characteristics and behavior.

Phishing Detection: Develop models that can recognize phishing attempts in email content and headers.

Insider Threat Detection: Monitor user activities for signs of insider threats, such as excessive access to sensitive data or unusual data transfers.

Machine learning, when integrated with Splunk, enhances your ability to detect and respond to advanced threats. It enables you to analyze large volumes of data quickly and identify patterns that might be too subtle for manual analysis. However, it's crucial to remember that machine learning is not a silver bullet; it should be used in conjunction with other threat detection techniques and human expertise to provide comprehensive security coverage.

Chapter 5: Threat Intelligence and APTs

In this chapter, we'll delve into the world of threat intelligence and examine how to leverage it to detect and respond to **Advanced Persistent Threats (APTs).** You'll learn about the top 10 known APT groups and understand what are **Indicators of Compromise (IoCs)**, as well as how to incorporate threat intelligence into your Splunk-based threat hunting activities.

5.1 What are Advanced Persistent Threats (APTs)?

Advanced Persistent Threats (APTs) are sophisticated and stealthy cyberattacks typically orchestrated by well-funded and highly skilled threat actors. APTs are characterized by their long-term focus, persistence, and ability to evade traditional security measures. They often target specific organizations or industries with the intent of espionage, data theft, or other malicious activities.

5.2 The Top 10 Known APT Groups

Let's explore the top 10 known APT groups as of my last knowledge update in September 2021:

APT1 (Comment Crew): A Chinese cyber espionage group known for stealing sensitive data from various industries.

APT28 (Fancy Bear): Linked to the Russian government, APT28 has been involved in various high-profile cyberattacks, including the 2016 U.S. presidential election interference.

APT29 (Cozy Bear): Another Russian-affiliated APT group, known for targeting government entities and think tanks.

APT32 (OceanBuffalo): Believed to be associated with the Vietnamese government, APT32 focuses on cyber espionage in Southeast Asia.

APT33 (Elfin): An Iranian APT group targeting critical infrastructure, particularly in the energy sector.

APT34 (OilRig): Engaged in cyber espionage activities on behalf of the Iranian government, APT34 targets organizations in the Middle East.

APT35 (Charming Kitten): Another Iranian APT group, known for phishing campaigns and espionage activities.

APT41 (Double Dragon): A Chinese APT group involved in both cyber espionage and cybercrime activities.

APT40 (Leviathan): An APT group linked to China, focusing on maritime and defense industries.

APT-C-23 (APT23): Associated with North Korea, this APT group has targeted various sectors, including media and entertainment.

5.3 Indicators of Compromise (IoCs)

IoCs are pieces of information that indicate potential security incidents or threats. Threat intelligence feeds provide valuable IoCs that can help identify APT activity within your network. Common IoCs include:

IP Addresses: Suspicious or known malicious IP addresses that have been associated with APT activity.

Domain Names: Suspicious domains or domains used for command and control servers.

File Hashes: Hash values of known malicious files or executables used by APTs.

Email Addresses: Email addresses used for phishing campaigns or communication with APT infrastructure.

URLs: Suspicious or known malicious URLs used in APT campaigns.

5.4 Using Threat Intelligence Feeds

To enhance your threat hunting capabilities, you can incorporate threat intelligence feeds into Splunk. Here's how:

Subscription to Threat Feeds: Subscribe to reputable threat intelligence feeds that provide IoCs related to APT activity.

Ingesting Threat Feeds: Configure Splunk to ingest threat intelligence data from these feeds.

Integration with Threat Feeds: Implement automated processes to correlate incoming data with threat intelligence and trigger alerts when matches are found.

Continuous Monitoring: Continuously monitor threat intelligence feeds to stay updated on the latest APT-related IoCs and tactics.

5.5 Incorporating Threat Feeds into Splunk

Integrating threat intelligence feeds into Splunk allows you to proactively detect APT activity:

Custom Searches: Craft custom Splunk searches that compare incoming data against threat intelligence feeds. For example, you can search for any inbound connections to known malicious IP addresses.

Alerting and Prioritization: Configure alerts to trigger when matches with threat intelligence IoCs are found. Prioritize alerts based on the severity and relevance of the IoCs.

Incident Response: Develop incident response procedures that include steps for handling APT-related alerts. This may involve isolating affected systems, collecting forensic data, and collaborating with threat intelligence providers.

By leveraging threat intelligence and understanding the tactics of known APT groups, you can bolster your organization's defenses and improve your threat detection capabilities using Splunk. In the following chapters, we'll explore more advanced threat hunting techniques and best practices for incident response and remediation.

To obtain IoCs associated with specific APT groups, you should consider the following steps:

Access Threat Intelligence Feeds: Subscribe to reputable threat intelligence feeds that specialize in tracking APT activity. These feeds often provide IoCs, such as IP addresses, domain names, file hashes, and more, associated with known APT campaigns.

Leverage Threat Intelligence Platforms (TIPs): Use threat intelligence platforms that aggregate and provide IoCs from various sources, making it easier to stay updated on APT-related threats.

Collaborate with Security Communities: Engage with the cybersecurity community, participate in information sharing forums, and collaborate with industry-specific Information Sharing and Analysis Centers (ISACs) to exchange threat information.

Utilize Commercial Threat Intelligence Services: Consider utilizing commercial threat intelligence services that offer comprehensive IoCs and reports on APT groups' activities.

Threat Hunting Tools: Employ threat hunting platforms and tools that integrate with threat intelligence feeds to automatically correlate IoCs with your network data.

Remember that IoCs are crucial for threat detection and response, but they should be used in conjunction with other security practices, such as network monitoring, log analysis, and anomaly detection, to provide a comprehensive defense against APTs and other threats. Additionally, the accuracy and relevance of IoCs can vary, so it's essential to validate them within the context of your organization's specific environment and security policies.

Chapter 6: Hunting for APTs

In this chapter, we will delve into the process of actively hunting for Advanced Persistent Threats (APTs) within your organization's network using Splunk. APTs are stealthy and sophisticated adversaries, so proactive threat hunting is crucial to identify and mitigate these threats before they cause significant damage. We'll explore practical examples and techniques for APT detection.

6.1 Understanding APTs and Their Tactics

Before diving into threat hunting, it's essential to understand APTs and their tactics. APT groups are typically state-sponsored or highly organized cybercriminal organizations that employ advanced techniques to infiltrate and maintain long-term access to target networks. Some common APT tactics include:

Spear Phishing: APTs often initiate attacks with highly targeted spear phishing emails to gain an initial foothold within an organization.

Lateral Movement: Once inside a network, APTs move laterally to explore and exploit vulnerabilities across different systems and segments.

Data Exfiltration: APTs aim to steal sensitive data, which may include intellectual property, customer data, or government secrets.

Persistence: APTs maintain access to a network for extended periods by installing backdoors, creating new accounts, or exploiting unpatched vulnerabilities.

Covering Tracks: APTs take steps to erase or hide their tracks, making detection more challenging.

6.2 Practical Examples of APT Hunting

Let's explore practical examples of APT hunting using Splunk. Each example focuses on detecting specific APT tactics or behaviors:

Example 1: Detecting Spear Phishing Attempts

Scenario: You want to identify **potential spear phishing attempts** targeting your organization's email accounts.

Step 1: Craft a Splunk Query

spl

index=email_logs sourcetype=email

| search subject="Invoice Payment Request" OR subject="Account Verification Required"

Step 2: Interpret the Results

This query searches email logs for emails with subject lines commonly used in spear phishing attempts.

Review the results to identify potentially malicious emails.

Example 2: Identifying Lateral Movement

Scenario: You suspect lateral movement within your network and want to detect unusual account activity.

Step 1: Craft a Splunk Query

spl

index=security_logs action="access"

| stats count by user, src_ip, dest_ip

| where count > 10

Step 2: Interpret the Results

This query searches security logs for access actions within your network.

It groups results by the **user, source IP, and destination IP addresses**.

The where **count > 10** filter identifies users with more than 10 access actions.

Review the results to identify unusual or excessive access behavior.

Example 3: Monitoring for Data Exfiltration

Scenario: You want to monitor for **data exfiltration** attempts by identifying large or unexpected data transfers.

Step 1: Craft a Splunk Query

spl

index=network_logs action="outbound" bytes_out > 10000000

_____

Step 2: Interpret the Results

This query searches network logs for **outbound traffic** with data transfers **exceeding 10 MB**.

Review the results to identify large or unexpected data transfers that may **indicate data exfiltration.**

Example 4: Detecting Persistence Mechanisms

Scenario: You want to detect signs of **persistence, such as newly created accounts or unusual service configurations.**

Step 1: Craft a Splunk Query

spl

index=system_logs sourcetype=security

| search "user created" OR "unusual service configuration"

_____

Step 2: Interpret the Results

This query searches system logs for events indicating the **creation of new user accounts** or **unusual service configurations.**

Review the results to identify **potential signs of persistence.**

Example 5: Covering Tracks

Scenario: You suspect that an **APT group is attempting to cover their tracks** within your network.

Step 1: Craft a Splunk Query

spl

index=security_logs sourcetype=logs

| search "log deletion" OR "event modification"

Step 2: Interpret the Results

This query searches security logs for events **indicating log deletion or modification.**

Review the results to identify any **suspicious log manipulation.**

6.3 Collaborating with Threat Intelligence

To enhance your APT hunting efforts, **collaborate with threat intelligence providers and subscribe to threat feeds that provide up-to-date IoCs and TTPs (Tactics, Techniques, and Procedures) associated with known APT groups.**

6.4 Incident Response

When you detect potential APT activity, it's essential to have a well-defined incident response plan in place. This plan should include steps for containment, eradication, recovery, and post-incident analysis. Splunk can play a vital role in incident response by providing real-time visibility and forensic data.

In conclusion, APT hunting is a proactive approach to cybersecurity

Chapter 7: Incident Response and Remediation

Incident response and remediation are critical components of cybersecurity, ensuring that when security incidents or breaches occur, organizations can effectively contain, investigate, and recover from them. In this chapter, we will explore the incident response process and how Splunk can be a valuable tool for managing and mitigating security incidents.

7.1 Incident Response Process

The incident response process typically consists of the following phases:

1. Preparation:

Develop an incident response plan (IRP) that outlines roles, responsibilities, and procedures.

Establish communication channels and contact information for key personnel.

Identify critical assets and data to prioritize protection and recovery efforts.

2. Identification:

Detect and identify security incidents by monitoring network traffic, logs, and alerts.

Utilize Splunk to correlate data and generate alerts for suspicious activities.

Classify incidents based on their severity and impact.

3. Containment:

Isolate affected systems or segments to prevent further compromise.

Utilize network segmentation, firewall rules, or access controls for containment.

Splunk can help track and document containment actions.

4. Eradication:

Investigate the root cause of the incident to eliminate vulnerabilities.

Analyze logs and system data to identify the initial attack vector.

Develop and implement strategies to remove malware and unauthorized access.

5. Recovery:

Restore affected systems to their normal operation.

Validate the effectiveness of eradication measures.

Monitor systems for signs of re-infection or recurrence.

6. Lessons Learned:

Conduct a post-incident review to analyze what went wrong and what went right during the incident response process.

Update incident response plans and security controls based on lessons learned.

7.2 Leveraging Splunk in Incident Response

Splunk can significantly aid incident response and remediation efforts:

Real-time Monitoring: Splunk's real-time monitoring capabilities allow security teams to detect incidents as they occur.

Log Analysis: Splunk can analyze logs and data from various sources to identify the scope and impact of an incident.

Alerting: Configure alerts in Splunk to notify incident responders when suspicious activities or known threats are detected.

Data Enrichment: Use Splunk to enrich incident data with threat intelligence feeds and contextual information.

Forensics and Investigation: Splunk's search and correlation capabilities help incident responders conduct in-depth investigations to determine the root cause of an incident.

Incident Documentation: Splunk can be used to document the entire incident response process, from detection to resolution, providing a comprehensive audit trail.

7.3 Case Study: Responding to a Data Breach

Let's explore a case study of incident response and remediation following a data breach using Splunk:

Scenario: An organization detects suspicious activity indicating a potential data breach. The incident response team uses Splunk to investigate and remediate the breach.

Phase 1: Identification

Splunk generates an alert based on anomalies in user access logs.

Security analysts investigate the alert and confirm unauthorized access to sensitive data.

Phase 2: Containment

The compromised user account is disabled immediately.

Affected systems are isolated from the network using firewall rules configured via Splunk.

Phase 3: Eradication

Splunk is used to analyze logs and trace the attacker's activities.

The root cause of the breach is identified as a phishing email that led to compromised credentials.

The phishing email is identified and deleted from all email accounts.

Phase 4: Recovery

Systems are restored from known clean backups.

Passwords for affected accounts are reset.

Continuous monitoring with Splunk ensures no further suspicious activity.

Phase 5: Lessons Learned

The incident response team reviews the incident and updates the security awareness training program to include phishing awareness.

New firewall rules are implemented to prevent similar attacks.

7.4 Proactive Incident Response with Automation

Splunk also supports automation in incident response. **Security orchestration and automation platforms (SOAR)** can be integrated with Splunk to automate incident triage, investigation, and response, allowing for faster and more consistent reactions to security incidents.

7.5 Continuous Improvement

Incident response is an ongoing process. Organizations should regularly review and update their incident response plans, conduct tabletop exercises, and stay informed about emerging threats and best practices in the field of cybersecurity.

In conclusion, effective incident response and remediation are vital for minimizing the impact of security incidents and breaches. Splunk, with its powerful log analysis and monitoring capabilities, can significantly enhance an organization's incident response capabilities, ultimately leading to a more resilient and secure environment.

Chapter 7.1: Incident Response and Remediation with Yara Rules

In this expanded chapter, we will delve into the integration of **Yara rules** into your incident response and remediation processes using Splunk. **Yara** is a powerful tool for identifying and classifying malware and suspicious files based on patterns and characteristics. By incorporating **Yara rules**, you can enhance your incident response capabilities, especially when dealing with malware-related incidents.

7.1 The Incident Response Process

Before we explore the integration of Yara rules, let's revisit the incident response process, which includes the following phases:

Preparation: Develop an incident response plan, establish communication channels, and identify critical assets.

Identification: Detect and classify security incidents through monitoring, alerts, and analysis.

Containment: Isolate and prevent further damage or unauthorized access.

Eradication: Identify and eliminate the root cause of the incident.

Recovery: Restore affected systems and services to normal operation.

Lessons Learned: Conduct a post-incident review to improve future responses.

7.2 Leveraging Yara Rules in Incident Response

Yara is a widely-used open-source tool for identifying and classifying malware based on patterns, characteristics, and behavioral indicators. Integrating Yara rules into your incident response process can be highly beneficial:

Yara Rule Creation: Security teams can create custom Yara rules to detect specific malware families or behaviors relevant to their organization.

Real-time Monitoring: Splunk can be configured to continuously monitor logs and data for matches with Yara rules, allowing for immediate detection of potentially malicious files or behavior.

Alerting: Custom alerts in Splunk can be triggered when Yara rules identify files or activities that match known malware characteristics.

Automated Actions: Upon detecting malware with Yara rules, automated actions can be initiated, such as isolating affected systems, blocking network traffic, or initiating malware removal procedures.

Incident Documentation: Splunk can be used to document the entire incident response process, including the use of Yara rules, providing a comprehensive audit trail.

7.3 Case Study: Using Yara Rules for Malware Detection

Let's explore a case study that illustrates the use of Yara rules in incident response:

Scenario: An organization detects unusual file behavior on a critical server, suspecting a malware infection. The incident response team uses Yara rules integrated with Splunk to identify and remediate the malware.

Identification:

Splunk generates an alert based on suspicious file behavior detected in server logs.

The incident response team creates a custom Yara rule to identify files associated with the suspected malware.

Real-time Monitoring and Alerting:

Splunk continuously monitors file activities and triggers alerts when the custom Yara rule matches potentially malicious files.

Containment and Eradication:

Upon an alert, automated actions are initiated to isolate the affected server from the network.

The incident response team uses Splunk to search for files that triggered the Yara rule and confirms the presence of malware.

Recovery:

Affected systems are taken offline and cleaned.

Malicious files are removed, and systems are restored from known clean backups.

Lessons Learned:

The incident response team reviews the incident and updates the **Yara rule library with new indicators of compromise (IoCs) from the malware infection.**

Additional Yara rules are created to proactively detect similar threats in the future.

7.4 Yara Rule Best Practices

When using Yara rules in incident response, consider the following best practices:

Regularly update Yara rules to include the latest IoCs and malware characteristics.

Use Yara rule sets tailored to your organization's specific environment and threat landscape.

Test Yara rules in a controlled environment to avoid false positives.

Ensure that your Yara rule infrastructure is well-documented and scalable for future needs.

7.5 Conclusion

The integration of Yara rules into your incident response and remediation processes can significantly enhance your organization's ability to detect and respond to malware-related incidents. By combining the power of Yara with Splunk's real-time monitoring and alerting capabilities, you can effectively identify and mitigate threats, minimizing the impact of security incidents and breaches on your organization.

Example uses of Yara rules:

Example: Detecting common windows executable with PE format

Yara rule that detects a common Windows executable file format (PE file) based on certain characteristics:

yara

rule Detect_PE_File {

meta:

description = "Detects a Windows PE (Portable Executable) file"

author = "Your Name"

strings:

$pe_magic = { 4D 5A } // The "MZ" magic bytes at the beginning of PE files

condition:

$pe_magic at 0

}

In this Yara rule example:

Detect_PE_File is the name of the rule.

meta provides metadata about the rule, such as its description and author.

strings define the byte sequences to search for in the file. Here, it looks for the "MZ" magic bytes that typically indicate the start of a Windows PE file.

condition specifies the condition that must be met for the rule to trigger. In this case, it triggers when it finds the "MZ" magic bytes at the beginning of the file.

You can customize Yara rules to detect specific malware families, file types, or behavioral patterns relevant to your organization's security needs. These rules can then be integrated into your incident response process to identify and respond to security incidents effectively.

Example 2: Detecting Malicious PowerShell Scripts

yara

rule Detect_Malicious_PowerShell {

meta:

description = "Detects potentially malicious PowerShell scripts"

author = "Your Name"

strings:

$script_signature = "IEX (New-Object Net.WebClient).DownloadString"

condition:

$script_signature

}

Use Case: This Yara rule is designed to identify potentially malicious PowerShell scripts commonly used in attacks. When integrated with an incident response system, it can trigger alerts when suspicious PowerShell activity is detected, allowing for prompt investigation and mitigation.

Example 3: Identifying Known Malware Families

yara

rule Detect_Malware_Family {

meta:

description = "Detects a specific known malware family"

author = "Your Name"

strings:

$malware_signature = "SomeUniqueStringInMalware"

condition:

$malware_signature

}

———

Use Case: This Yara rule can be used to detect a specific known malware family by searching for unique strings or patterns associated with that malware. When integrated with an incident response system, it helps in quickly identifying and responding to known threats.

Example 4: Detecting Web Shell Backdoors

yara

rule Detect_Web_Shell {

meta:

description = "Detects common web shell backdoors"

author = "Your Name"

strings:

$web_shell_signature = "eval(base64_decode("

condition:

$web_shell_signature

}

Use Case: This Yara rule is designed to identify common web shell backdoors that attackers often deploy on compromised web servers. When integrated into a web server's security monitoring, it helps in identifying and removing unauthorized access points.

Example 5: Finding Suspicious Email Attachments

yara

rule Detect_Suspicious_Email_Attachment {

meta:

description = "Detects suspicious email attachments"

author = "Your Name"

strings:

$suspicious_attachment = { 25 50 44 46 2D } // Detects common file headers, e.g., PDF

condition:

$suspicious_attachment

}

Use Case: This Yara rule is useful for identifying suspicious email attachments based on their file headers. Integrating this rule into an email security system can help prevent malicious attachments from reaching users' inboxes.

These Yara rule examples demonstrate the flexibility and versatility of Yara in detecting a wide range of threats, from malicious scripts and malware families to web shell backdoors and suspicious email attachments. By incorporating Yara rules into your security infrastructure and incident response processes, you can strengthen your organization's defenses against cyber threats.

Chapter 8: Threat Intelligence and Threat Sharing

In this chapter, we will explore the importance of threat intelligence and threat sharing in enhancing your organization's cybersecurity posture. Threat intelligence provides valuable insights into emerging threats and vulnerabilities, while threat sharing promotes collaboration and knowledge exchange among organizations to better defend against cyberattacks.

8.1 Understanding Threat Intelligence

Threat intelligence refers to the knowledge and insights derived from analyzing cybersecurity threats and vulnerabilities. It provides organizations with information about potential risks, attacker tactics, and indicators of compromise (IoCs) that can be used to detect and respond to security incidents. Threat intelligence can be categorized into three main types:

Strategic Threat Intelligence: High-level information that helps organizations understand the broader threat landscape, including emerging threats, threat actors, and their motivations.

Operational Threat Intelligence: Tactical information used by security teams to identify and mitigate specific threats, such as IoCs and attack techniques.

Technical Threat Intelligence: Detailed technical data, such as malware signatures, IP addresses, and file hashes, used for immediate threat detection and response.

8.2 The Value of Threat Intelligence

Threat intelligence provides several key benefits to organizations:

Early Threat Detection: By staying informed about emerging threats, organizations can detect and respond to threats more quickly, reducing the impact of security incidents.

Enhanced Situational Awareness: Threat intelligence helps organizations gain a better understanding of the threat landscape, enabling more informed decisions about security measures.

Proactive Defense: Armed with threat intelligence, organizations can proactively implement security controls and strategies to mitigate known threats.

Incident Response Improvement: Threat intelligence enriches incident response efforts, helping analysts identify the root cause of incidents and develop effective mitigation strategies.

8.3 Leveraging Splunk for Threat Intelligence Integration

Splunk can play a crucial role in integrating threat intelligence into your organization's security operations:

Threat Feed Integration: Configure Splunk to ingest threat intelligence feeds, which may include IoCs, indicators of attack (IoAs), and context-rich information about threats.

Enrichment: Use Splunk to enrich your logs and data with threat intelligence, adding context to security events and alerts.

Correlation: Splunk's search and correlation capabilities allow you to correlate threat intelligence data with your network and system logs to identify potential threats.

Alerting: Create custom alerts in Splunk that trigger when events match known threat intelligence indicators, enabling rapid response.

Reporting and Visualization: Splunk's reporting and visualization features help security teams present threat intelligence data effectively to stakeholders.

8.4 Threat Sharing and Collaboration

Threat sharing involves the exchange of threat intelligence and information about security incidents among organizations, government agencies, and industry groups. Collaborative threat sharing has several advantages:

Collective Defense: Organizations can benefit from the collective knowledge and experience of the community to defend against threats collectively.

Early Warning: Threat sharing allows organizations to receive early warnings about emerging threats that may not have affected them yet.

Mitigation Strategies: Sharing threat intelligence can help organizations develop and implement effective mitigation strategies based on the experiences of others.

Regulatory and Compliance Requirements: Some industries and regulations require organizations to participate in threat sharing as part of their cybersecurity measures.

8.5 Threat Intelligence Sharing Platforms

Several threat intelligence sharing platforms and organizations facilitate the exchange of threat information, including:

Information Sharing and Analysis Centers (ISACs): Industry-specific organizations that facilitate the sharing of cyber threat information among members.

Government Agencies: Many countries have established government-run threat sharing initiatives to enhance national cybersecurity.

Commercial Threat Intelligence Providers: Companies that offer threat intelligence services and platforms for organizations to subscribe to.

8.6 Case Study: A Threat Intelligence-Driven Defense

Let's explore a case study of how an organization leverages threat intelligence and threat sharing to enhance its cybersecurity defenses:

Scenario: A financial institution receives threat intelligence indicating an increase in attacks targeting banking credentials. The organization uses this intelligence to bolster its defenses.

Threat Intelligence Integration:

The organization configures Splunk to ingest threat intelligence feeds, including known malicious IP addresses and phishing URLs.

Real-time Monitoring and Alerting:

Splunk continuously monitors network traffic and logs for matches with the threat intelligence indicators.

Custom alerts trigger when the organization's systems communicate with malicious IP addresses or access phishing URLs.

Incident Response:

When an alert is triggered, the incident response team uses Splunk to investigate the incident promptly.

The threat intelligence data helps identify the attack vector and tactics used by the attackers.

Threat Sharing:

The organization shares its findings and threat intelligence with an ISAC focused on the financial sector.

In return, the organization receives information about new threats targeting the financial industry.

Security Enhancements:

Based on threat intelligence and lessons learned from threat sharing, the organization updates its security controls, implements stronger email filtering, and enhances user awareness training.

8.7 Conclusion

Threat intelligence and threat sharing are essential components of a robust cybersecurity strategy. By integrating threat intelligence into your Splunk environment and participating in collaborative threat sharing efforts, you can stay ahead of evolving threats and enhance your organization's ability to detect, respond to, and mitigate security incidents.

Chapter 9: Security Automation and Orchestration with Splunk

In this chapter, we will explore the concepts of security automation and orchestration (SOAR) and how you can leverage Splunk as a central component to streamline and enhance your security operations. SOAR allows organizations to automate repetitive security tasks, respond to threats more efficiently, and orchestrate complex incident response workflows.

9.1 Understanding Security Automation and Orchestration

Security Automation and Orchestration (SOAR) is a set of technologies and practices that enable organizations to automate, coordinate, and optimize their security processes. SOAR platforms integrate with various security tools and technologies to facilitate the automation of tasks, such as alert triage, incident response, and threat hunting.

Key components of SOAR include:

Orchestration: The ability to coordinate and sequence security tasks and actions across multiple tools and teams.

Automation: The use of scripts, workflows, and playbooks to automate repetitive security tasks and responses.

Incident Response: Rapidly and efficiently responding to security incidents, minimizing their impact.

Integration: Connecting with various security tools, data sources, and APIs to gather and share information.

9.2 Benefits of SOAR with Splunk

Integrating Splunk into your SOAR strategy offers several advantages:

Centralized Data: Splunk serves as a centralized platform for collecting and analyzing security data from various sources, making it an ideal hub for SOAR activities.

Real-time Visibility: Splunk provides real-time visibility into security events and incidents, enabling faster decision-making and response.

Customization: Splunk's flexibility allows you to tailor automation and orchestration workflows to your organization's specific needs.

Threat Intelligence Integration: Incorporate threat intelligence feeds into Splunk and automate actions based on real-time threat indicators.

9.3 Use Cases for SOAR with Splunk

Let's explore practical use cases for implementing SOAR with Splunk:

Use Case 1: Automated Alert Triage

Scenario: Splunk generates numerous security alerts daily. Many of these alerts are false positives, causing alert fatigue among analysts.

SOAR Solution: Implement an automated alert triage process that leverages machine learning and custom scripts. Splunk can analyze alert data, prioritize alerts based on risk, and automatically validate or dismiss low-risk alerts, allowing analysts to focus on high-priority incidents.

Use Case 2: Incident Response Playbooks

Scenario: When a security incident is detected, the incident response process involves numerous manual steps, leading to delays in containment and remediation.

SOAR Solution: Develop incident response playbooks that integrate Splunk with other security tools and automate actions such as isolating affected systems, gathering forensic data, and notifying stakeholders. These playbooks can be triggered automatically or by analysts.

Use Case 3: Threat Hunting Automation

Scenario: Security analysts want to proactively hunt for threats using Splunk but are overwhelmed by the sheer volume of data.

SOAR Solution: Create threat hunting automation scripts that use predefined queries in Splunk to continuously search for indicators of compromise (IoCs) and suspicious patterns. When potential threats are detected, automated actions or alerts can be initiated.

Use Case 4: Patch and Vulnerability Management

Scenario: Splunk identifies vulnerable systems in the network, but patching and remediation are often delayed.

SOAR Solution: Implement a patch and vulnerability management workflow that integrates with Splunk. When vulnerabilities are identified, the SOAR platform can trigger automated patching or mitigation actions based on predefined policies.

9.4 Challenges and Considerations

While SOAR with Splunk offers significant benefits, there are challenges to consider:

Complexity: Implementing SOAR solutions can be complex and may require specialized expertise.

Integration: Ensure seamless integration with existing security tools and data sources.

False Positives: Be cautious about over-automation, which can lead to false positives and missed threats.

Data Privacy: Consider data privacy and compliance regulations when automating responses.

9.5 The Future of Security Automation and Orchestration

SOAR is continually evolving to keep pace with the changing threat landscape. The future of SOAR with Splunk may involve:

Machine Learning and AI: Enhanced use of machine learning and artificial intelligence to improve automation, threat detection, and decision-making.

Cloud Integration: Integration with cloud-native security tools and platforms for comprehensive security coverage.

Behavioral Analytics: Leveraging behavioral analytics to detect sophisticated and evolving threats.

Community Collaboration: Enhanced collaboration among security professionals and organizations for threat intelligence sharing and playbook development.

9.6 Conclusion

Security automation and orchestration with Splunk empower organizations to respond to security incidents more effectively, reduce response times, and improve overall cybersecurity posture. By implementing SOAR solutions that integrate seamlessly with Splunk, you can streamline your security operations, enhance threat detection and response, and better protect your organization against cyber threats.

Chapter 10: Compliance Monitoring and Reporting with Splunk

In this chapter, we will explore how Splunk can be effectively utilized for compliance monitoring and reporting. Compliance with industry standards and regulations is crucial for organizations to maintain the security and integrity of their data. Splunk provides powerful tools for collecting, analyzing, and reporting on security and compliance-related data.

10.1 The Importance of Compliance

Compliance refers to an organization's adherence to specific industry standards, regulations, or internal policies governing data security, privacy, and operational practices. Compliance is critical for several reasons:

Legal Obligations: Many industries and regions have legal requirements for data protection and privacy.

Data Integrity: Compliance measures help ensure the integrity of sensitive data, reducing the risk of data breaches.

Reputation Management: Maintaining compliance helps protect an organization's reputation and customer trust.

Operational Efficiency: Compliance can streamline processes and improve operational efficiency.

10.2 Splunk's Role in Compliance Monitoring

Splunk can play a central role in compliance monitoring by:

Data Collection: Splunk can collect and index data from various sources, including logs, databases, and network traffic, ensuring comprehensive coverage of compliance-relevant information.

Real-time Monitoring: Splunk's real-time monitoring capabilities allow organizations to detect compliance violations as they occur.

Custom Reporting: Splunk enables the creation of custom compliance reports and dashboards, simplifying the reporting process.

Alerting: Organizations can set up automated alerts in Splunk to notify them of potential compliance breaches or anomalies.

10.3 Common Compliance Frameworks and Regulations

There are several compliance frameworks and regulations that organizations often need to adhere to, including:

PCI DSS (Payment Card Industry Data Security Standard): Applies to organizations handling credit card data.

HIPAA (Health Insurance Portability and Accountability Act): Pertains to healthcare organizations and the protection of patient data.

GDPR (General Data Protection Regulation): Regulates the protection of personal data for individuals within the **European Union (EU).**

ISO 27001: An international standard for **information security management systems (ISMS).**

SOX (Sarbanes-Oxley Act): Mandates regulations on financial reporting for publicly traded companies in the United States.

10.4 Compliance Monitoring Use Cases with Splunk

Let's explore practical use cases for implementing compliance monitoring with Splunk:

Use Case 1: PCI DSS Compliance Monitoring

Scenario: An e-commerce company must adhere to **PCI DSS** to protect customer credit card data.

Splunk Solution: Set up real-time monitoring of payment processing logs, perform regular vulnerability scans, and generate PCI DSS compliance reports to ensure adherence.

Use Case 2: HIPAA Compliance Monitoring

Scenario: A healthcare provider must comply with **HIPAA** to safeguard patient data.

Splunk Solution: Implement **data loss prevention (DLP) solutions** and use Splunk to monitor access logs, generate audit trails, and create alerts for potential violations of patient data privacy.

Use Case 3: GDPR Compliance Monitoring

Scenario: An international organization must comply with GDPR to protect EU citizens' personal data.

Splunk Solution: Use Splunk to track and report on data access and consent, manage data subject requests, and monitor for data breaches that may impact GDPR compliance.

10.5 Automating Compliance Reporting

Splunk can automate the compliance reporting process by:

Creating Compliance Reports: Use Splunk's reporting capabilities to generate compliance reports with customized data visualizations.

Scheduling Reports: Schedule automatic report generation at specified intervals and distribute them to relevant stakeholders.

Automated Alerts: Set up automated alerts for potential compliance violations, ensuring timely response.

Audit Trails: Maintain detailed audit trails to demonstrate compliance efforts to auditors and regulators.

10.6 Continuous Compliance Improvement

To maintain compliance effectively, organizations should focus on continuous improvement by:

Regular Auditing: Conduct regular audits of systems, processes, and data handling practices.

Training and Awareness: Provide ongoing training and awareness programs to ensure employees understand and adhere to compliance requirements.

Threat Monitoring: Continuously monitor for security threats and vulnerabilities that could impact compliance.

Updates: Keep abreast of changes in compliance regulations and update policies and procedures accordingly.

10.7 Conclusion

Compliance monitoring and reporting are critical aspects of modern organizations, helping them protect sensitive data, maintain legal and regulatory requirements, and build trust with customers and partners. Splunk's capabilities for data collection, real-time monitoring, custom reporting, and automation make it an invaluable tool for achieving and maintaining compliance across a variety of frameworks and regulations. By leveraging Splunk's features, organizations can streamline their compliance efforts and ensure ongoing adherence to the highest standards of data security and privacy.

———

Conclusion: Mastering Security and Compliance with Splunk

In this comprehensive guide, we've embarked on a journey through the realms of cybersecurity, threat hunting, incident response, compliance monitoring, and more, all powered by the exceptional capabilities of Splunk. Our exploration has revealed how Splunk, a versatile and robust platform, serves as a cornerstone in fortifying an organization's defenses and ensuring regulatory adherence.

From the foundations of cybersecurity in Chapter 1, where we delved into the principles of security and the evolving threat landscape, to the practical application of Yara rules and threat intelligence sharing in Chapters 8 and 9, we've uncovered the tools and strategies required to safeguard digital assets.

Splunk's pivotal role in this journey became evident as we explored its diverse features:

Real-time monitoring, alerting, and log analysis to detect threats as they emerge.

The power of automation and orchestration in Chapter 7, empowering us to respond to incidents swiftly and decisively.

Chapter 10 highlighted Splunk's contribution to compliance monitoring, helping organizations navigate the complex landscape of regulations and frameworks.

We've not only understood the theory but also witnessed Splunk in action through numerous practical examples and use cases. Whether it was crafting Yara rules for malware detection, automating incident response, or ensuring GDPR compliance, Splunk has proven its mettle as a versatile and indispensable tool for security professionals.

As the cybersecurity landscape continues to evolve, and new threats emerge, the importance of a robust security strategy and the right tools cannot be overstated. Splunk, with its real-time data analysis, custom reporting, and automation capabilities, stands as a sentinel against the ever-advancing forces of cybercrime.

In the realm of compliance, Splunk provides organizations with the means to not only meet the requirements of regulatory bodies but also to maintain the trust of customers and partners. The ability to generate compliance reports, schedule audits, and monitor data in real-time positions organizations to stay ahead of compliance challenges.

In conclusion, this guide has provided you with a solid foundation for mastering security and compliance with Splunk. But remember, cybersecurity is an ongoing journey, and the threat landscape is in a constant state of flux. To remain vigilant, organizations must continuously adapt, update their security strategies, and harness the power of tools like Splunk to protect their digital assets, ensure compliance, and ultimately, thrive in an increasingly digital world.

Appendix: Useful Resources for Splunk Security and Compliance

In this appendix, we've compiled a list of useful resources to further your knowledge and expertise in using Splunk for security and compliance:

1. Splunk Documentation:

Splunk's official documentation provides comprehensive guidance on using the platform for various purposes, including security and compliance. You can find detailed information, tutorials, and best practices.

Website: Splunk Documentation

2. Splunk Blogs:

Splunk maintains a blog that covers a wide range of topics related to security, compliance, and data analysis. It's a valuable source of insights, case studies, and industry trends.

Website: Splunk Blogs

3. Splunk Answers:

Splunk Answers is a community-driven platform where users can ask questions, share knowledge, and find solutions to common issues. It's an excellent resource for troubleshooting and learning from other users' experiences.

Website: Splunk Answers

4. Splunkbase:

Splunkbase is the official marketplace for Splunk apps, add-ons, and custom visualizations. You can find and download security-related apps and add-ons to extend Splunk's capabilities.

Website: Splunkbase

5. Splunk Education:

Splunk offers a range of training courses and certifications, including those focused on security and compliance. These courses are designed to help you become a Splunk expert.

Website: Splunk Education

6. Splunk Community:

The Splunk Community is a place where users, administrators, and developers can collaborate, share knowledge, and discuss various topics related to Splunk.

Website: Splunk Community

7. Security and Compliance Apps:

Explore the Splunk App for Enterprise Security, which is designed for security professionals and provides advanced security monitoring, detection, and response capabilities.

Website: **Splunk App for Enterprise Security**

8. Compliance Frameworks and Regulations:

To dive deeper into specific compliance frameworks and regulations like PCI DSS, HIPAA, and GDPR, consult the official documentation and resources provided by the respective regulatory bodies and organizations.

9. Books on Splunk:

Consider reading books dedicated to Splunk, its use cases, and best practices in security and compliance. Look for titles available through online retailers and bookstores.

10. Splunk Webinars and Events:

- Splunk frequently hosts webinars and events related to security, compliance, and data analysis. These events provide insights from experts and real-world use cases.

- Website: **Splunk Events**

11. Security and Compliance Forums:

- Explore online forums and communities dedicated to security, compliance, and Splunk. These platforms offer discussions, Q&A sessions, and shared experiences.

12. Security and Compliance Consultants:

- If your organization requires specialized assistance with security and compliance, consider consulting with professionals or organizations that specialize in Splunk implementations and security consulting services.

These resources will help you expand your knowledge, troubleshoot issues, and stay up-to-date with the latest trends and best practices in using Splunk for security and compliance. Whether you're just starting your journey or seeking advanced expertise, these references will prove invaluable in mastering Splunk for your organization's security and compliance needs.

Appendix B: Glossary of Terms

This glossary provides definitions for key terms and acronyms used throughout this guide:

Alert: A notification generated by a security system or monitoring tool indicating a potential security event or anomaly.

APT (Advanced Persistent Threat): A sophisticated and prolonged cyberattack orchestrated by well-funded and skilled adversaries, typically targeting specific organizations.

Compliance: Adherence to established regulations, industry standards, and internal policies governing data security, privacy, and operational practices.

Cybersecurity: The practice of protecting computer systems, networks, and data from unauthorized access, breaches, and damage.

Data Breach: Unauthorized access, acquisition, or disclosure of sensitive data, often resulting in data loss or exposure.

Incident Response: The process of detecting, managing, and mitigating security incidents and breaches.

IOC (Indicator of Compromise): A piece of information, such as an IP address, domain name, or file hash, that suggests a system or network has been compromised.

Malware: Malicious software designed to infiltrate, damage, or gain unauthorized access to computer systems or networks.

Phishing: A cyberattack method that involves tricking individuals into revealing sensitive information, such as login credentials, by posing as a trustworthy entity.

SIEM (Security Information and Event Management): A comprehensive security solution that combines security information management (SIM) and security event management (SEM) to provide real-time analysis and correlation of security events.

SOC (Security Operations Center): A centralized facility that monitors and manages an organization's security posture and responds to security incidents.

Splunk: A versatile data analysis and visualization platform used for monitoring, analyzing, and responding to data across various sources, including security logs.

Threat Actor: An individual or group responsible for launching cyberattacks or engaging in malicious activities.

Threat Intelligence: Information about potential threats, vulnerabilities, and attack techniques that helps organizations identify and defend against cybersecurity threats.

Yara: An open-source tool for identifying and classifying malware and suspicious files based on patterns and characteristics.

Zero-Day Vulnerability: A software vulnerability or security flaw that is exploited by attackers before the software vendor releases a patch or fix.

SOAR (Security Orchestration, Automation, and Response): A set of technologies and practices that automate and orchestrate security tasks and incident response processes.

DLP (Data Loss Prevention): A strategy and technology used to prevent the unauthorized transmission or leakage of sensitive data outside an organization.

GDPR (General Data Protection Regulation): European Union regulation that governs the protection and privacy of personal data for individuals within the EU.

PCI DSS (Payment Card Industry Data Security Standard): Security standards that apply to organizations handling credit card data to prevent fraud and data breaches.

HIPAA (Health Insurance Portability and Accountability Act): U.S. legislation governing the protection of patient healthcare data and privacy.

ISO 27001: An international standard for information security management systems (ISMS) that provides a systematic approach to managing information security risks.

SOX (Sarbanes-Oxley Act): U.S. legislation that sets regulations and standards for financial reporting and corporate governance.

Please refer to this glossary for clarification on terms and acronyms encountered in the guide. If you come across additional terms or concepts that require explanation, consult relevant industry-specific sources and resources for further information.

Index

A

Alert: A notification generated by a security system or monitoring tool indicating a potential security event or anomaly.

APT (Advanced Persistent Threat): A sophisticated and prolonged cyberattack orchestrated by well-funded and skilled adversaries, typically targeting specific organizations.

C

Compliance: Adherence to established regulations, industry standards, and internal policies governing data security, privacy, and operational practices.

Cybersecurity: The practice of protecting computer systems, networks, and data from unauthorized access, breaches, and damage.

D

Data Breach: Unauthorized access, acquisition, or disclosure of sensitive data, often resulting in data loss or exposure.

I

Incident Response: The process of detecting, managing, and mitigating security incidents and breaches.

IOC (Indicator of Compromise): A piece of information, such as an IP address, domain name, or file hash, that suggests a system or network has been compromised.

M

Malware: Malicious software designed to infiltrate, damage, or gain unauthorized access to computer systems or networks.

P

Phishing: A cyberattack method that involves tricking individuals into revealing sensitive information, such as login credentials, by posing as a trustworthy entity.

S

SIEM (Security Information and Event Management): A comprehensive security solution that combines security information management (SIM) and security event management (SEM) to provide real-time analysis and correlation of security events.

SOC (Security Operations Center): A centralized facility that monitors and manages an organization's security posture and responds to security incidents.

Splunk: A versatile data analysis and visualization platform used for monitoring, analyzing, and responding to data across various sources, including security logs.

T

Threat Actor: An individual or group responsible for launching cyberattacks or engaging in malicious activities.

Threat Intelligence: Information about potential threats, vulnerabilities, and attack techniques that helps organizations identify and defend against cybersecurity threats.

Y

Yara: An open-source tool for identifying and classifying malware and suspicious files based on patterns and characteristics.

Z

Zero-Day Vulnerability: A software vulnerability or security flaw that is exploited by attackers before the software vendor releases a patch or fix.

Disclaimer:

The information provided in this e-book is intended for educational and informational purposes only. While every effort has been made to ensure the accuracy and reliability of the content, the author and publisher do not make any representations or warranties regarding the completeness, accuracy, or suitability of the information contained herein. The author and publisher shall not be liable for any loss, damage, or injury arising from the use or reliance on the information presented in this e-book.

Readers are encouraged to seek professional advice and conduct their own research to make informed decisions regarding their Splunk security practices. Any reliance on the information provided in this e-book is at the reader's own risk.